Peter and the Wolf

Story by Sergei Prokofiev

Retold by Annette Smith

Illustrated by Naomi Carolyn Lewis

Once upon a time, a boy named Peter
lived with his grandfather
in a small wooden cottage
at the edge of a dark forest.

In front of the cottage
was a beautiful, green meadow.
Peter liked to play in the garden
around the cottage,
but he longed to go into the meadow.

Grandfather would say to him,
"Stay near the house, Peter.
Never, never go into the meadow.
It is a very dangerous place!"

"Why is the meadow dangerous?" asked Peter.

"There is a fierce wolf in the forest!" replied his grandfather.
"It could sneak into the meadow and attack you."

3

For a long time,
Peter remembered his grandfather's words.
However, one day, a little bird
flew down to the tree by the garden.
"Come out into the meadow,"
she chirped.
"All is quiet! All is quiet!"

Peter forgot about his grandfather's warning.
He pushed the gate open
and ran out into the meadow.

The little bird flew around his head.
She darted and swooped,
and Peter followed her down to the pond.

A fat white duck waddled out of the reeds.
She was pleased to see Peter.

But the little bird
wasn't pleased to see the duck.
"What sort of bird are you?"
she chirped.
"You can't even fly!"

"Well," answered the duck,
"what sort of bird are you?
You can't even swim!"

The bird and the duck
were making so much noise
that they didn't hear the big gray cat
creeping through the long grass
behind them.

But Peter had seen the cat.
"Look out!" he yelled
to the bird and the duck.

The duck swam to the middle
of the pond,
and the little bird flew up
into the branches of a tree.

Peter's grandfather heard the noise
and hurried out of the cottage.
When he saw the gate was open,
and that Peter was out in the meadow,
he was very angry indeed.

"Come here at once, Peter,"
he said sternly.

So Peter went back inside the garden,
and Grandfather went back
inside the cottage.

Meanwhile, the hungry wolf
had been watching them
from the edge of the forest.

Just in time, the cat saw the wolf
and raced up the tree to save herself.
She sat on a branch not far
from the little bird.

The wolf crept closer and closer
to the pond.

The duck quacked in fright.
She jumped out of the pond,
and the wolf raced after her.
She had no way of escaping,
and the wolf swallowed her
in one mouthful.

The wolf began to walk
around and around the tree.
He looked up at the cat
and the little bird
with his greedy yellow eyes.

Peter saw what was happening.
He wasn't scared of the wolf.
He got a long piece of rope.
Then he climbed up onto the garden wall
and crawled along a branch of the tree.

Once he was settled on a bigger branch,
he made a loop in one end of the rope.
"Fly around the wolf's head,"
Peter called to the little bird,
"and try to make him dizzy."

The little bird darted around the wolf, making sure she kept just out of reach of his sharp teeth.

Peter dropped the rope down.
The loop went over the wolf's tail.
With a quick flick,
Peter pulled the rope tight
and tied the other end to the tree.
He had caught the wolf!

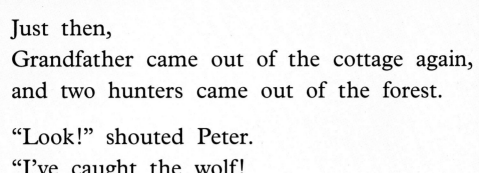

Just then,
Grandfather came out of the cottage again,
and two hunters came out of the forest.

"Look!" shouted Peter.
"I've caught the wolf!
Please come and help me
take him to the zoo."

So they all set off,
with Peter leading the way.
The hunters followed him
carrying the wolf in a net.
Grandfather and the cat came along behind.
And the little bird flew above them all
singing happily, "Peter and I caught the wolf!"